HIDDEN DANGER

The strong jaws of the alligator snapping turtle could easily bite off your finger. Luckily, it prefers to eat fish, tempting them into its mouth with a built-in worm on its tongue. There are over 200 species of freshwater turtles living at the bottom of lakes, rivers and swamps. They can stay underwater for long periods and can even hibernate there for weeks at a time.

SNORKELS, AQUALUNGS AND GILLS

Finding ways of obtaining oxygen is vital for aquatic animals to survive. Hanging upside-down from the surface of the water, mosquito larvae take oxygen from the air through a 'snorkel' at the rear end of their body. Other methods of obtaining oxygen include the 'aqualungs' or bubbles of air carried underwater by diving beetles, and the gills of fish, tadpoles and damselfly larvae, which allow oxygen from the water to enter directly into the animal's body.

WETLAND PEOPLES

Many people live near rivers, lakes and swamps so they can use them for water, food and transport. In this floating market in Thailand, people sell their fruit, vegetables and other produce from boats. This is because the houses there have canals of water flowing past them instead of roads. Waterways all over the world provide vital links for trade and transport.

SUPER DIVER

In fast-flowing water and strong currents, many animals and plants have adaptations that stop them being swept away. The torrent duck has no problem diving into the foaming, rushing waters of rivers in the Andes to look for insect larvae to eat. It uses sharp hooks under its wings to cling to slippery rocks, while balancing and steering with its stiff tail. Its large webbed feet make it a powerful swimmer.

WETLANDS OF THE WORLD

LAKE BAIKAL

The deepest and oldest lake in the world is Lake Baikal in Siberia. It is at least 25 million years old and bigger than Belgium. It contains the world's largest volume of freshwater – more than that of North America's five Great Lakes put together. Lake Baikal contains a huge variety of wildlife. More than 1,000 of the species that live there are found nowhere else in the world.

Wetlands are areas of land that are covered by water. Wetlands make up about six per cent of the Earth's surface, ranging from tiny mountain streams to vast flooded forests called swamps. They are found all over the world, wherever there is heavy rainfall or where water stays on the surface because it cannot drain away. Wetlands occur in every type of climate, including the frozen Arctic; the hot tropical rainforests; and the temperate regions in-between. The Okavango wetland even survives among the sands of the Kalahari Desert. Wetlands are often found along coasts, such as the mangrove swamps of tropical coasts or the saltmarshes of river estuaries. There are huge areas of wetland on the lands drained by giant rivers. Wetlands are always changing as lakes and ponds dry up or fill in with plants, and saltmarshes or mangrove swamps gradually extend out to sea.

NORTH AMERICA

KEY

▨ Wetland areas of the world

Areas mentioned in this book

1   Lake Baikal, Russia
2   The Camargue, France
3   The Okavango Delta, Botswana
4   The Amazon, Brazil
5   Malaysian Mangroves
6   Boglands of Europe
7   Sunderbans, Bangladesh
8   The Everglades, USA
9   Lake Victoria, E. Africa
10 Lake Tanganyika, E. Africa
11 Lake Nakuru, E. Africa
12 Norfolk Broads, Britain
13 Kakadu N.P. Australia
14 Coto Doñana, Spain

THE CAMARGUE

The famous white Camargue horses live on the salty marshes and shallow lakes of the River Rhône estuary in France. They eat a lot of marshland reeds and so stop the reeds spreading across areas of water close by. This is lucky for tens of thousands of swans, ducks and geese, as these waters provide food, winter homes and resting places during their migration.

MALAYSIAN MANGROVES

Mangrove swamps run along the coasts of Malaysia and other tropical countries, holding together the sticky mud with their roots. There is little oxygen in the mud, so the mangroves take it from the air through their roots. A whole army of creatures live in mangrove swamps.

EUROPE   ASIA   ❶

❿   ❷

⓮

AFRICA

ATLANTIC OCEAN

❾❿⓫

❸

INDIAN OCEAN

PACIFIC OCEAN

❺

❼

⓭   AUSTRALIA

❻

⓬

THE AMAZON RIVER

The Amazon is the second largest river in the world and holds more than 25 per cent of the Earth's freshwater. About 2,000 species of fish live in the Amazon, as well as many reptiles, such as caimans and anacondas, and mammals such as the manatee. When the Amazon floods, its waters create a huge area of flooded forest the size of England. This swamp forest, called igapo, is flooded for four to seven months of the year, and rises up to a height of 12 metres (40 ft).

THE OKAVANGO DELTA

Stretching over 20,000 sq km (7,700 sq miles) of the Kalahari Desert, in Botswana, the Okavango Delta provides an oasis for wildlife. It is home to hippos, crocodiles, lechwe, sitatunga and thousands of water birds, such as ducks, geese, herons, ibises and fish eagles. In the dry season, desert antelope mingle with wetland species such as waterbuck.

WETLAND PLANTS

AIR PLANTS

The silvery bubbles on the leaves of this Canadian pondweed are oxygen bubbles. The bubbles occur when the plant makes its food in a process called photosynthesis. There are more bubbles on sunny days because the plant needs the Sun's energy, along with water and carbon dioxide, to make its food. Carbon dioxide in the water is taken in through the leaves of the plants. Canadian pondweed provides oxygen for plants and animals to breathe but it spreads quickly and can choke other plants.

Hundreds of plants grow in the wetlands, from algae, mosses and water lilies to reeds, grasses and trees. The water supports the weight of the plant, so they do not need strong stems, like plants on land. Water and nutrients float around the plants in the water, so their roots are usually small and either float or anchor the plant in the mud. They also do not have to live through such extreme temperatures as land plants. There are some disadvantages though. Oxygen and light are sometimes hard to come by and producing seeds and flowers can be difficult, especially in times of flood or drought.

WATER POLLINATION

A few plants, such as ribbon weed, rely on water for pollination. This is a more risky process than pollination by insects.

1. Ripe male flowers float up to the surface of the water. They have a bubble of air inside them to help them float.

2. Male flowers are pushed along by the wind and water currents, and slide down into the female flower.

3. Once the female flower has been pollinated, it is pulled back under the water by the flower stalk.

4. Under the water, the pollinated flower ripens into a fruit, protected by the leaves.

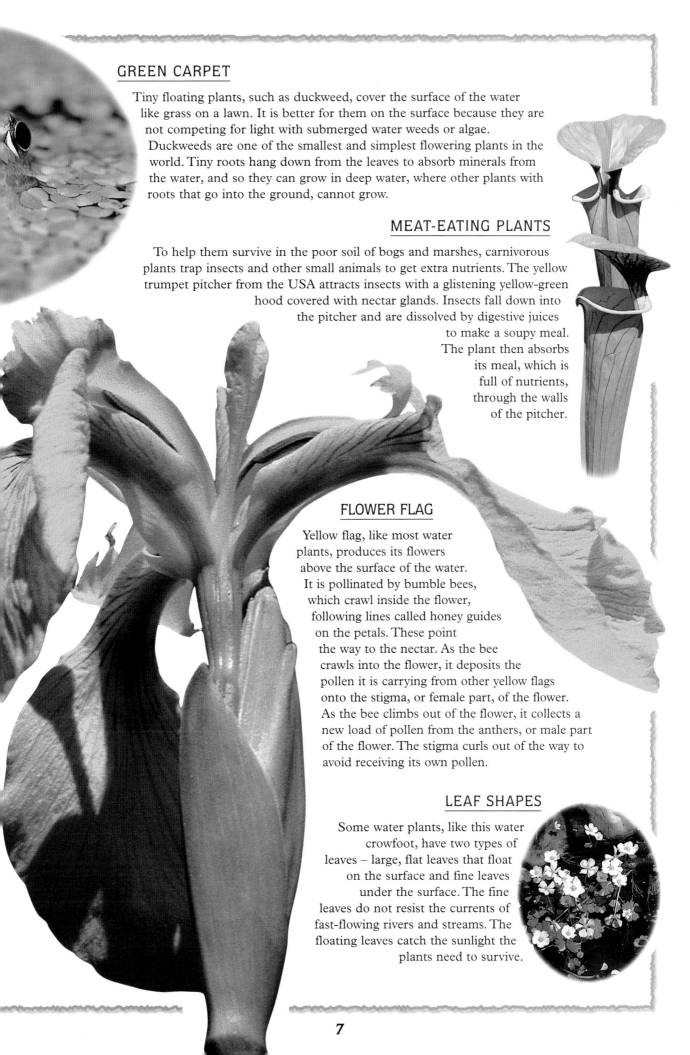

GREEN CARPET

Tiny floating plants, such as duckweed, cover the surface of the water like grass on a lawn. It is better for them on the surface because they are not competing for light with submerged water weeds or algae. Duckweeds are one of the smallest and simplest flowering plants in the world. Tiny roots hang down from the leaves to absorb minerals from the water, and so they can grow in deep water, where other plants with roots that go into the ground, cannot grow.

MEAT-EATING PLANTS

To help them survive in the poor soil of bogs and marshes, carnivorous plants trap insects and other small animals to get extra nutrients. The yellow trumpet pitcher from the USA attracts insects with a glistening yellow-green hood covered with nectar glands. Insects fall down into the pitcher and are dissolved by digestive juices to make a soupy meal. The plant then absorbs its meal, which is full of nutrients, through the walls of the pitcher.

FLOWER FLAG

Yellow flag, like most water plants, produces its flowers above the surface of the water. It is pollinated by bumble bees, which crawl inside the flower, following lines called honey guides on the petals. These point the way to the nectar. As the bee crawls into the flower, it deposits the pollen it is carrying from other yellow flags onto the stigma, or female part, of the flower. As the bee climbs out of the flower, it collects a new load of pollen from the anthers, or male part of the flower. The stigma curls out of the way to avoid receiving its own pollen.

LEAF SHAPES

Some water plants, like this water crowfoot, have two types of leaves – large, flat leaves that float on the surface and fine leaves under the surface. The fine leaves do not resist the currents of fast-flowing rivers and streams. The floating leaves catch the sunlight the plants need to survive.

PEAT BOGS

Large areas in cooler parts of the world are covered in soggy, flat peat bogs (or mires) and fenlands. These places are types of wetlands, but wetlands with waterlogged, peaty soil, that have taken 5,000 years to form. Bogs occur in Canada, Russia and most of Europe, especially Finland. The peat is formed when dead plant material only partly decomposes in the wet soil. This can happen around the edge of a lake or on ground where the rainfall is heavy and the rocks are hard and acidic. Few plants grow in these acidic conditions, although carnivorous plants, cotton sedges and cranberries are common. Waterlogged bogs are perfect for aquatic insects and biting flies, which in turn are eaten by birds and frogs. Many birds nest on peat bogs, including snipe, redshank, curlews, merlins, short-eared owls and even golden eagles.

VACUUM CLEANERS

Bladderworts have small sacs on their thin, underwater leaves. If aquatic insects brush against these sacs, a trap door bursts open. Water is then sucked into the sac, carrying the insect with it. The bladderwort's trap works rather like a botanical vacuum cleaner.

MIRACLE MOSS

The most common peat bog plant is sphagnum moss. This amazing bright green, bushy moss soaks up water like a huge bath sponge. It can absorb up to ten times its own weight in water. In the past, it was used on soldier's wounds and American Indians used dried sphagnum moss as nappies for babies. Today, it is used by gardeners in their hanging baskets to stop water from draining away too quickly. Sphagnum moss sucks nutrients out of the water and on peat bogs it makes the water even more acidic.

BOG BIRDS

Many wader birds, such as this curlew, nest in bogs because there are plenty of safe nesting sites and insects to eat. The mother and young are both well camouflaged to blend in with the vegetation and the fluffy chicks can run about as soon as they hatch. Birds also use peat bogs as winter resting places or feeding areas during migration journeys.

STICKY FLYPAPER

A fly provides a tasty snack for this sundew plant. Special hairs on the leaves have sticky droplets on the ends. Insects are attracted to the droplets and stick fast to the leaves. As the fly struggles, the leaf folds round it and pours digestive juices over the fly's body. The plant can then absorb goodness from the fly's body. After a day or so, all that is left of the fly is a dry, empty shell. The leaf then straightens out again, ready to catch its next meal.

HOW A PEAT BOG FORMS

A peat bog may form when a lake fills in with mud and plants.

The water is clear, with mud on the bottom of the lake.

Silt and mud collect around plant roots. This build-up allows plants to grow across the lake.

Mosses grow, die and start to rot, building up layers of peat.

Bog mosses build up domes of peat above the level of the water. This is called a raised bog.

BOG BODIES

Over 1,000 ancient bodies have been found preserved in peat bogs in northern Germany, Scandinavia and Britain. The acidic conditions and low levels of oxygen in the bogs stopped the bodies from decomposing. Oxygen is needed for something to decompose because the bacteria that break down plant and animal material need oxygen to survive. The acidic peat preserves so well, that it was possible to identify the last meal of a 2,000-year-old body, found in the peat.

RIVER ANIMALS

When a river flows from the mountains to the sea, its moving water provides a number of places for animals to feed and shelter. Insect larvae, worms, water snails and shrimps living on the riverbed are eaten by fish, crayfish and turtles. The fish in turn, are hunted by otters, crocodiles and birds; such as herons, dippers and kingfishers. Swallows and bats swoop low over the water to scoop up insects hatching on the water's surface. The moving water of rivers holds more oxygen for animals to breathe than the still water of ponds and lakes. But river animals must avoid being washed away by the current or smashed against the rocks. They hide away in crevices, glue themselves to rocks, or cling on tightly with hooks and suckers. In some rivers, muddy water may make it difficult for animals to find or catch food. Some animals, such as salmon and eels, spend only part of their life cycle in rivers, moving to the sea to breed or feed.

FLYING
UNDERWATER

The dipper has the amazing ability to walk underwater up the beds of fast-flowing streams to search for water insects, tadpoles and worms. Its tail helps it move in the current and keeps its feet firmly on the bottom. It also dives into the water from the air. A hunting dipper means that the water is clean. If pollution kills the insects that it feeds on, the dipper cannot survive.

SPECTACULAR
SALMON

Salmon make long migration journeys from their feeding grounds in the sea to their breeding grounds in rivers. They usually return to the river where they themselves hatched, by recognising the distinctive smell of the water. As they journey upriver, the salmon may have to leap up waterfalls. They make their best jumps from deep water because they can build up speed beforehand. Many jumps fail though and the salmon drop back exhausted.

STREAMLINED HUNTER

The shy otter is a land animal that spends much of its time in the water, particularly when feeding. Its fur is waterproof. An otter hunts for eels, trout and crayfish from dusk to dawn, finding its prey by sight or using its whiskers to sense the vibrations made by fish as they swim. For slow swimming, the otter moves its webbed feet in a dog-paddle. For greater speed, the otter holds its legs close to the body and moves its whole body up and down. The flattened tail acts as a rudder.

LIFE IN THE FAST LANE

A leech has two suckers, which it uses to cling onto stones or water plants so it is not swept away by the current. Other adaptations for fast-flowing waters include the hooks of blackfly larvae and the flattened bodies of crayfish, flatworms, stonefly nymphs and mayfly nymphs. Some caddis fly larvae make cases around their bodies and stick themselves to stones or weight their cases down with pebbles.

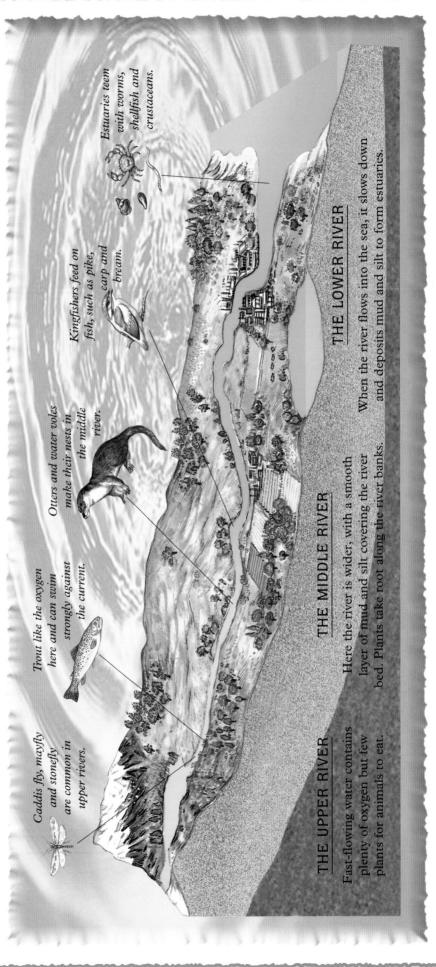

Estuaries teem with worms, shellfish and crustaceans.

Kingfishers feed on fish, such as pike, carp and bream.

Otters and water voles make their nests in the middle river.

Trout like the oxygen here and can swim strongly against the current.

Caddis fly, mayfly and stonefly are common in upper rivers.

THE UPPER RIVER

Fast-flowing water contains plenty of oxygen but few plants for animals to eat.

THE MIDDLE RIVER

Here the river is wider, with a smooth layer of mud and silt covering the river bed. Plants take root along the river banks.

THE LOWER RIVER

When the river flows into the sea, it slows down and deposits mud and silt to form estuaries.

LAKE & POND DWELLERS

The still waters of lakes and ponds are complex ecosystems, where conditions change with the seasons, the climate and the water levels. There is a delicate balance of life in these still waters, which is easily changed through pollution. Pollution such as sewage and fertilizers encourage algae to grow, which blocks out the light and uses up oxygen. In a clean pond or lake, there are three main zones: the pelagic zone of deep water in the middle, with algae, plankton and fish; the benthic zone at the bottom, with algae, worms, larvae, and molluscs; and the littoral zone around the edge, with reeds, rooted plants and animals. Deeper lakes usually contain fewer animals than shallow ones but a greater variety of species. Lakes and ponds may freeze over in the winter but the wildlife survives in a layer of cold water trapped under the ice.

DIVING BELL

The water spider is the only spider which spends its whole life underwater. It cannot breathe oxygen from the water, so it lives inside a bell-shaped web of silk, which it fills with air. It takes up to six trips to and from the surface to fill the silken bell with air. The spider eats, mates and lays its eggs inside the bell. It only leaves the bell to catch food and find a mate.

FEATHERED FISHERMAN

The large and powerful great blue heron of North America often stands still at the edge of ponds and lakes watching for fish or frogs to come close. It may also stalk its prey, before using its long, sharp bill to spear, or to hold onto its prey. Most of these herons migrate south to warmer places in the winter.

WOOD DUCK

The beautiful colours of the male wood duck contrast with the camouflaged greys and browns of the female. Wood ducks live in lakes and ponds in wooded areas and nest in tree cavities. After hatching, the young jump from the nest to the ground and follow their mother to the water.

POND MAKER

Beavers create ponds around their homes, called lodges, by building a dam of sticks and stones across a river. Their dams may be as tall as a person and up to 100 metres (328 ft) long. A beaver's pond is rather like a moat around a castle, helping to keep away predators, such as wolves and bears. A beaver can also use its pond to float logs and branches to the lodge and the dam.

UNIQUE SPECIES

Lakes are often home to unique species that are cut off from others of their own kind. Lake Victoria and Lake Tanganyika in East Africa are home to hundreds of different species of cichlid fish, like these guarding their nest from a terrapin (right). The different species can live together because they are adapted to eating different kinds of food.

FILTERING FLAMINGOS

Flamingos wade into salty lakes to find algae, small plants and animals from the water. They trap the food with comb-like plates on the bill. Flamingos live in large colonies, sometimes containing thousands of birds. They form a spectacular, but smelly, sea of pink on lakes such as Lake Nakuru in East Africa.

LOUDMOUTH GATORS

Alligators are the largest reptiles in North America and also the loudest; the males bellowing particularly loudly in the breeding season. The sound carries for long distances, warning other males to keep away and telling females where they are. Alligators dig out large holes in the Everglades, which fill with water that helps wildlife in the dry season. The alligators also feed on the wildlife, such as turtles and fish, sheltering in their gator holes.

RARE EGRET

This reddish egret hunts fish, frogs and crabs in the shallows of Florida Bay at low tide. It lurches, twists and turns through the shallows, dashing to the left and right in hunting its prey. Egrets, herons and ibises were hunted in the 1880s to supply feathers for the luxury hat trade. In the 20th century, the birds have been threatened by changing water levels, which destroys their nesting and feeding areas.

SPOON FEEDING

Nesting colonies of roseate spoonbills are a spectacular sight in the Everglades. They are named after their strange, spoon-shaped bill, which they use to find food in the muddy waters of the Everglades. They feed on small fish, shrimps and shellfish, snapping their bills shut when they touch their prey.

PRECIOUS PANTHER

Southern Florida is the last known refuge in the Eastern United States for the cougar – known in this area as the Florida panther. This beautiful predator is a powerful and expert hunter, jumping up to 6 metres (20 ft) in a single bound. The Florida panther needs a large territory in which to hunt mammals, such as deer. Although the Everglades is big, it may not be big enough to save the species. There are probably only about 30-50 animals left in the wild.

THE EVERGLADES

At the southern tip of Florida in the USA is a huge area of cypress swamp, mangroves and marsh called the Everglades. This famous wetland covers a massive area of 5,490 sq km (2,120 sq miles) yet is only just above sea level. In the summer, higher water levels allow animals to move freely through the park. In the winter, they gather around the few remaining water holes. At least 300 types of bird, 25 mammals and 60 types of reptile can be found in the Everglades. The birds feed on the variety of insects and fish that live in this warm, humid environment. Several rare animals have taken refuge in the Everglades but, sadly, the park is threatened on all sides by farming, buildings and people.

UNITED STATES
OF AMERICA

THE EVERGLADES

MUDDY MANGROVES

Where the Everglades meets the sea, mangrove swamps occur. Mangroves are remarkable trees that are adapted to live in wet, salty places. Breathing pores in their roots take in oxygen from the air and help them to survive in waterlogged mud with little oxygen. Red mangroves like these protect the coast from storms and strong waves. They trap mud with their roots and new areas of land build up around them.

NESTING PREDATOR

The fish-eating osprey is a resident of the Everglades. Its bulky nest is built on dead trees, floating buoys and telephone poles in the Florida Bay area or the mangrove wilderness. Ospreys are well adapted for catching fish, with sharp spines on their feet to grip hold of their slippery prey. They plunge feet-first into the water, grasping the fish in their strong talons.

MARSHES & SWAMPS

The difference between a marsh and a swamp is that a marsh is a wet grassland, while a swamp is a waterlogged forest with specially adapted trees, such as swamp cypress or mangroves. These amazing places are part land and part water. They are usually found along the edges of lakes, reservoirs, ponds, rivers or oceans where the waters become clogged with mud and the smell of rotting plants is everywhere. Aquatic worms and crabs move slowly through the soft, slushy mud and water snails feed on the stems and leaves of water plants. The shallow, protected waters of swamps and marshes provide ideal homes for baby fish, tadpoles, insect larvae and the young of shellfish and shrimps. They are also an important feeding and breeding area for waterbirds, reptiles and mammals. Swampy areas act as natural reservoirs, collecting water in the rainy season and releasing it during the dry season.

SWAMP STORKS

The magnificent saddle-bill stork is Africa's largest stork. It is named after the yellow 'saddle' on its upper bill. This long, pointed bill makes a handy weapon for stabbing fish and other prey in the water. Its big feet disturb the fish as it wades through the water.

STRIPY SWIMMER

Several hundred tigers live in the Sundarbans, an enormous soggy swamp on the western edge of the Ganges, Brahmaputra and Megha river deltas in Bangladesh. The name Sundarbans means 'beautiful forest'. Dotted through the swamp are about 50 muddy islands covered with tropical forest, much of it underwater at high tide. The tigers hunt swamp deer, pigs, fish and crabs and share their swamp with a rich variety of animals, including crocodiles and monkeys.

AIR PLANTS

Hanging from the trees like long hair, Spanish moss is one of the best-known air plants in the Everglades swamp of Florida. Air plants, called epiphytes, grow on other plants and take their nourishment from the air. Despite its name, Spanish moss is a member of the pineapple family – the bromeliads. There are also rare epiphytic orchids in the Everglades as well as epiphytic vines and ferns.

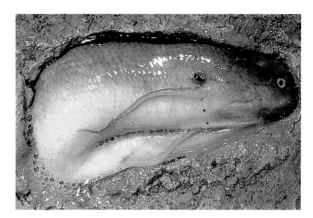

SUMMER SIESTA

Some lungfish survive drought by going into a type of summer hibernation called aestivation. As the water level falls, the fish burrows into the soft mud and secretes a mucus cocoon around its body. The cocoon stops moisture evaporating from the fish's body and the lungfish breathes air through the lid of the cocoon. During aestivation, the body slows down so the lungfish uses very little energy. Some lungfish have survived up to four years this way.

SCARCE SWALLOWTAIL

In Britain, the lovely swallowtail butterfly survives only in a man-made marsh, the Norfolk Broads. This was created by the flooding of old peat pits, which were excavated in the Middle Ages. The caterpillars of the swallowtail eat milk parsley plants, which vary in number each year. Many caterpillars are eaten by spiders, birds and small mammals. High water levels in the Norfolk broads need to be maintained if the swallowtail is to survive.

WATERY MOVEMENT

Many small water creatures float or drift through the water, letting the water currents or wind push them along. Fish, frogs, water beetles and other larger animals use their muscles to move through the water. Water is much denser than air, so it supports an animal's weight but also holds it back as it tries to swim along.

To make swimming easier, aquatic animals have a smooth, streamlined shape, a slippery surface and often, webbed feet. On the surface of the water is a thin invisible 'skin', like a springy, bouncy platform. This skin is formed of water molecules that are attracted to each other and stick tightly together. To enable them to move on this surface skin, creatures, such as pond-skaters, have special adaptations, such as waxy feet and long legs to spread their weight.

WATER WALKER

Unlike small insects that really do walk on water, the African jacana, or lily-trotter, cheats by walking on floating lily pads instead. Its big feet, with their long, thin toes, work like the long legs of pond-skaters. They spread out the weight of the lily-trotter over a wide area and stop it sinking down into the water.

FROGGY PADDLE

At the first sign of danger, an adult frog will leap into the water. It can move faster through water than it can on land and there are plenty of places to hide among the water plants. The long, slim body of a frog make it a streamlined shape for cutting through the water easily. Its webbed back feet are like the flippers we wear when snorkelling or diving. They push a lot of water out of the way so the frog can swim fast.

HAIRY OARS

Water boatmen
are water bugs
that live in
ponds, canals
and ditches.
They have a
streamlined,
boat-shaped
body and long,
powerful back
legs, which
stick out of the
sides of the body
like oars. Hairs
on the legs help
brush the water aside
as the insect moves
through the water.

UNDERWATER TANK

Looking rather like a giant
underwater tank, the hippopotamus
lumbers along the bottom of rivers,
lakes and swamps. It is an excellent
swimmer and diver and can stay
underwater for up to five minutes.
Hippos spend most of the daytime
in the water because their skin loses
water easily and they would dehydrate
quickly in the hot African sun. They
are well adapted for an aquatic life.
Water flows easily over their smooth
skin, their webbed toes act like
paddles. They can close their nostrils
and ears to keep the water out when
they are underwater.

BLUE JEWEL

Kingfishers are shy birds, usually seen as a flash of bright
blue speeding like an arrow along the river.
To catch fish, the kingfisher dives headfirst into the water.
Sometimes it will hover before diving. Once in the water
(right), the kingfisher spears its prey with its dagger-like
beak and holds it firmly until it gets back to the perch.
There it beats its prey against a hard surface and swallows
it headfirst. This makes sure the fish's fins and scales do
not get caught in the bird's throat.

ALGAE

WATER FLEA

STICKLEBACK

PERCH

HERON

*Fish-eating
waterbirds such as
herons, kingfishers and
storks are often the top
predators
at the end of
wetland food chains.
But these food
chains often include
more than one fish
and the big fish gobble
up the smaller ones.*

PREDATORS & PREY

MASKED BANDIT

Mischievous raccoons use their long, nimble fingers for finding and catching aquatic prey, such as crayfish, fish, frogs and clams. They tend to rub, feel and dunk their food in water, perhaps to get rid of nasty skin secretions. Raccoons are more active in the evening than in the daytime and are good swimmers and climbers. The name raccoon comes from *arahkunem*, a Native American name for the animal. It means 'he scratches with his hands'.

Wetlands are full of tasty meals for predators to eat, especially water insects and fish. The biggest predators include alligators, crocodiles, anacondas, tigers and fish eagles. Some predators, such as snakes and otters, hunt in the water. Others, such as bats and fish eagles, swoop down to snatch a meal from the water's surface. Different techniques for catching prey include the surprise ambush of a crocodile, the high-speed chase of an otter, the stealthy stalk of a tiger or the tricky trap of a Venus flytrap plant. Mammals, such as otters and bats, together with reptiles, such as alligators and snakes, tend to hunt under cover of darkness. Birds, however, are daytime hunters. To catch and kill their prey, wetland predators rely on weapons such as sharp bills, teeth and talons as well as poisons and electric shocks.

PRISON BARS

The Venus flytrap is the most spectacular hunting plant, living only in one small patch of marshy country in Carolina, North America. Insects are attracted to the trap by its colour or the sweet nectar below the spikes. If they brush against hairs on the surface of the trap, the two halves snap shut in under half of a second. The walls of the trap press tightly together and digestive juices dissolve the insect's body.

SHOOTING INSECTS

The remarkable archerfish spits drops of water from the surface of the water to shoot down insects sitting on leaves above. If the insect falls into the water, the archerfish can snap it up. If the fish is only a few centimetres from the insect, it will jump out of the water and snatch the insect with its jaws rather than shoot it down.

FISHING EAGLE

The national bird of the USA, the bald eagle, is a predator of fish, birds and small mammals. It swoops down to the surface of the water to snatch fish in its strong talons. Groups of bald eagles gather at salmon spawning grounds in Alaska, where the large number of dead and exhausted fish provide easy meals. This eagle is named after the white feathers on its head – an old meaning of the word bald.

FISHING SPIDER

Sitting on floating leaves or twigs with their front legs resting on the surface of the water, fishing spiders lie in wait for their prey. Hairs on their legs detect ripples in the water caused by fish swimming nearby. The spider can work out the position of a fish from the direction of the ripples and the distance between them. They kill their prey with a poisonous bite.

NORTH AMERICAN FOOD CHAIN

ALGAE

MOSQUITO LARVAE

BLUEGILL

FLORIDA SPOTTED GARFISH

ALLIGATOR

Wetland food chains rely on tiny floating plants in the water, which provide food for a variety of water insects. These, in turn, feed fish, which are preyed on by larger predators such as alligators and snakes.

DEFENCE

From armour and camouflage to poisons and chemical weapons, wetland animals use a number of strategies to stay alive. For shoals of fish, flocks of waterbirds, herds of antelope or families of beavers there is safety in numbers. But many animals prefer to hide among the water plants, such as under lily pads or in-between the reeds along the water's edge. The sitatunga, an African antelope, submerges itself under the water if it senses danger, with only the tip of its nose showing above the surface. Frightening enemies is another survival tactic. Some animals display coloured markings, while snakes or crocodiles may hiss and puff up their bodies with air so they look bigger and more scary. Chemical weapons include poisons secreted by the skin of toads and salamanders, and acids sprayed by some caterpillars. Coming out at night helps some creatures, such as eels and moths, to avoid their predators.

FLASH COLOURS

Fire-bellied toads have undersides which are boldly marked with bright red, orange or yellow but the tops of their bodies are camouflaged with grey or green colours. To confuse a predator, the toads suddenly expose their bright colours, giving themselves time to escape. The bright belly colours warn of poisonous skin secretions.

THE NUMBERS GAME

By keeping together, this shoal of minnows can help one another to spot danger. They also have less chance of being singled out for attack. Predators find shoals of fish confusing targets and most of the fish escape an attack.

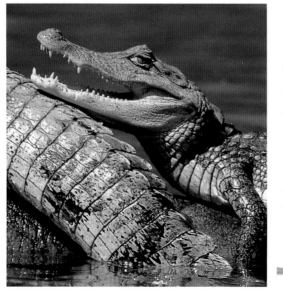

CHAIN MAIL

The outside of crocodiles, alligators and caimans bodies are covered in tough scales and bony plates set into the thick, leathery skin. This armour is rather like the coat of chain mail worn by medieval knights. Few predators will risk attacking a well-armoured adult crocodile, with its sharp teeth and powerful jaws. The crocodile's main enemy is people, who kill them for their skins, for food, or because they are dangerous.

CLEVER CAMOUFLAGE

Bitterns build their nests among reeds where they are well hidden and protected from enemies. These shy and secretive birds are very difficult to see in their marsh habitat. When threatened, a bittern often 'freezes' with its bill pointing straight up to the sky. The lines on its breast feathers look just like the reeds and it may even sway back and forth, like reeds in the wind.

HARMLESS HOGNOSE

The hognose snake of North America is harmless but it makes itself look frightening to scare away predators. First it widens its neck into a cobra-type hood. Then it hisses loudly and strikes towards the enemy. If all *that* does not work, the hognose snake smears itself all over with smelly scent and then rolls over and pretends to be dead. Predators prefer to eat live prey, so they leave the hognose snake alone.

SHELL SECURITY

Water snails can withdraw their bodies inside their hard shells for protection. The operculum, or door, to the shell can be closed to make a watertight seal. A snail's shell is secreted from a part the body wall called the mantle and is made of calcium salts taken from the water. The large shell of the great pond snail needs a lot of calcium carbonate so this species can only thrive in water containing plenty of lime.

NESTS, EGGS & YOUNG

PECULIAR PLATYPUS

The Australian duck-billed platypus is a very unusual mammal that lays eggs instead of giving birth to live young. The female lays two eggs at the end of a special breeding tunnel in a river bank, out of sight of predators. She curls herself around the eggs and incubates them for up to 14 days. The baby platypuses cut their way out of their eggs with an egg tooth. They feed on their mother's milk, which oozes out of her belly onto her fur.

The thick and rich plant growth in wetlands habitats provide safe places for animals to lay eggs, build nests and give birth. The shallow water areas contain plenty of food for the young animals to eat and calm water in which they can practise their swimming skills. Huge colonies of breeding birds, such as flamingos and herons, are found in wetlands. Some animals, such as frogs and dragonflies, spend part of their lives in the water and part on land. The eggs are laid in the water and the young develop there, but the adults move to new wetland areas. This helps new populations grow and prevents chance disasters wiping out whole populations.

A DOUBLE LIFE

Struggling to pull itself free of its larval skin, an adult dragonfly is about to begin its life as a hunter in the air. Eventually, it will mate and the female will lay her eggs in the water. The eggs hatch into larvae, which live underwater for between one and five years. The nymphs (young) breathe through gills on the tips of their abdomens and feed mainly on aquatic invertebrates. They shed their skins several times as they slowly grow into adults.

REED BASKET

The reed warbler's nest is like a basket, fixed between dry reed stems above the wet reed bed. The nest is held in place with 'handles' and both male and female birds add grass, feathers and flowers on top to build up the nest. Reed warblers need considerable skill to stay in the nest, because the reeds constantly sway about in the wind.

NESTING COUPLE

The male stickleback encourages a female to swim through his nest of waterweeds and lay her eggs. Then he will also swim through the nest and fertilise the eggs with his sperm. The male guards the nest closely, chasing away enemies and fanning oxygen-rich water over the eggs with his front fins. Even after the young hatch, the male stickleback still keeps watch over his family, picking them up in his mouth if they stray too far away.

FLAMINGO MILK

To make sure their chicks get enough food, flamingo parents produce a rich 'milk' in their crop – a kind of pouch in the wall of the gut. The milk is bright red because it contains red pigment from the food the birds eat. Their feathers also become pink or red for the same reason. When chicks are hungry, they make begging calls. Their beaks are straight at first and they have fluffy feathers to keep them warm. Older chicks gather into a crèche and are guarded by the adults in turn while other adults go off to feed.

LIVING TOGETHER

Animals often live in a group to help each other look out for danger and take care of their young. A large source of food can cause animals, such as crocodiles, to group together. A drought can force groups to gather at water holes or any last source of water. Herons, egrets, storks and other wetland birds, gather together to nest in large colonies. Other animals, such as shoals of fish or herds of antelope or horses, live together all year round. Mammal societies often have a leader, such as a male zebra, leading a group of females and their young. Other family groups in wetlands include otter and beaver families. Sometimes, different kinds of animals live together and help each other to survive.

CROCODILE GATHERINGS

Crocodiles gather together in groups to bask in the sun, share food, court each other and nest. Groups, called pods, of young crocodiles hang out together and warn each other of danger. In times of drought, crocodiles of all ages gather together to share the water and avoid competing for food. Dominant crocodiles defend territories, which contain mates, feeding places, nests and dens.

ZEBRA HERDS

Splashing across the Okavango swamplands in Africa, these Burchell's zebras protect themselves from predators by sticking together. Zebras live in family groups made up of females and their young, led by a strong male. Rival males will fight each other for control of a herd of females. The zebras communicate by means of sounds or body language, such as moving the position of the ears or the tail. Several families share an area and may join in large herds, but family members can always recognise each other by voice, scent and the pattern of their stripes.

PIRANHA PACKS

Packs of red-bellied piranhas hunt through the tropical rivers of South America. In a matter of minutes they can strip the flesh off animals as large as goats, that have accidentally fallen into the water. Meat-eating piranhas only turn to eating meat when plant food is hard to find. For most of the year they live on fruit and nuts that fall into the water.

PLANT LODGERS

The pitcher plants of bogs sometimes have animals living inside their pitchers. This one has a small tree frog sitting at the top, waiting to snap up insects before they fall down into the living trap. The pitcher has developed a small chamber in its stem that is regularly used by ants. As they steal a meal from the bottom of the pitcher, the ants accidentally help to chop up the pitcher's food.

HIPPO HERDS

During the day, hippos stay in the water in groups of 10 or 15, made up of all-male bachelor groups or nursery groups. The nursery groups contain females and their young within the territories of a dominant male. In the evenings, the aquatic groups break up and the animals go ashore to feed. Other animals sometimes live with hippos, such as these oxpeckers that are feeding on tiny creatures on this hippo's skin.

PEOPLE & WETLANDS

People use wetlands in many ways – for fishing, farming, transport, tourism and sport. The reeds from marshes are used for thatching roofs or to make houses and boats. The peat from bogs can be burned as fuel, or used as garden soil. Transporting goods and people by water is still important in many parts of the world. Many people live near rivers and lakes and rely on them for their water supply. The energy from flowing water can also be used to make electricity. This is called hydroelectric power – 'hydro' means water. Unexpected floods can cause terrible problems for people living near rivers, such as the Mississippi in North America or the Huang Ho in China.

PEAT CUTTING

These men are cutting blocks of peat on the Outer Hebrides in Scotland to burn for fuel. They are using a special spade with a long handle and a thin blade, but peat is also dug with bulldozers and large mechanical diggers. Peat pieces are cut by hand and stacked to allow them to dry before they are used. Peat is used to supply soil for gardens as well as for fuel. About 96 per cent of Britain's peat bogs have been destroyed in the last 150 years. As well as affecting the wildlife, digging up peat releases carbon dioxide into the atmosphere and speeds up global warming.

BOAT TRAFFIC

Zooming through a North American swamp on an airboat is fun, but it disturbs the wildlife more than using boats without engines, such as canoes. The propellers from airboats can also injure wildlife, such as manatees in the Florida Everglades. Boat engines cause a lot of pollution and noise and the wash from boats can drown the eggs and chicks of birds nesting in the vegetation on the water's edge.

CROCODILE PEOPLE

The crocodile plays an important part in the myths and legends of the Iatmul people of the Sepik River in New Guinea. The saltwater crocodile was common in the mangrove swamps of the Sepik River and is believed by some peoples to be the creator of all living things. Its skull is kept in the men's spirit houses, such as this one, and the initiation ceremony for the young men involves cutting their skin to look like the scales of a crocodile.

FLOODED FIELDS

In Asia, artificial wetlands are created when people flood fields to farm rice, which grows best when the plants are grow in waterlogged mud. These flooded fields are called paddy fields and can also be used to farm frogs or fish, sometimes in pools next to the fields. This farmer is herding his geese across a rice paddy. People have grown rice in Thailand, China and India for at least 5,000 years.

CORMORANT FISHING

For centuries, cormorants have been used by people to help them catch fish. A ring is placed around the bird's neck to prevent it from swallowing the fish. When the cormorant comes to the surface, it is hauled to the boat on a special perch and the fish are taken out of its mouth. Later, the ring is removed so the cormorant can feed itself. Experienced birds can be trained to fish without the ring.

PROTECTING WETLANDS

NATURE RESERVES

The Camargue wetland in France is protected as a National Park but it is surrounded by cities. Pollution seeps into the park wetlands, and large numbers of tourists may frighten and disturb the wildlife. Illegal hunting also goes on in the park. So even though a wetland may be protected, it still has to be managed very carefully, taking into account problems caused outside the protected area.

Wetlands are important places for wildlife, supporting about 10 per cent of all the world's species. They are useful to people in all sorts of ways, as well as having a vital effect on the environment around them. Wetlands can help to control flooding by soaking up heavy rainfall and releasing the water slowly. Mangrove swamps protect coasts from soil erosion and the effect of storms. In some places, wetlands also act as a form of natural pollution control, filtering the water that flows through them and removing the pollutants. On a global scale, peat bogs 'lock up' the carbon dioxide released from burning coal and oil and so help reduce global warming. However, about half the wetlands that once existed have disappeared and those that remain urgently need our protection if they are to survive in the future. But leaving wetlands alone is not enough – their water supply has to be carefully controlled.

MINING PROBLEMS

The Ranger uranium mine, on the edge of Kakadu National Park in Australia's Northern Territory, digs up uranium for nuclear energy. Kakadu is a World Heritage Site of rivers, flood plains, creeks and billabongs (stagnant pools of water) spread over an area the size of Wales. It is home to many rare and unique species which are threatened by the presence of the mine.

CLEANING-UP WETLANDS

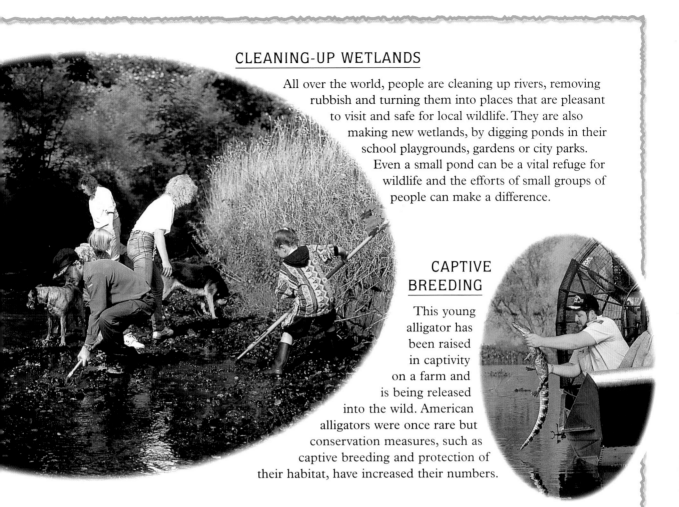

All over the world, people are cleaning up rivers, removing rubbish and turning them into places that are pleasant to visit and safe for local wildlife. They are also making new wetlands, by digging ponds in their school playgrounds, gardens or city parks. Even a small pond can be a vital refuge for wildlife and the efforts of small groups of people can make a difference.

CAPTIVE BREEDING

This young alligator has been raised in captivity on a farm and is being released into the wild. American alligators were once rare but conservation measures, such as captive breeding and protection of their habitat, have increased their numbers.

RIVER MANAGEMENT

People build dams across rivers to control flooding, provide a water supply and generate electricity. But the dam changes the amount of water and sediment in the river and creates a huge artificial lake behind the dam. There may not be enough water downstream for people, farms, plants or animals. Changing the natural course of a river may actually cause flooding and other problems in the long term.

RARE SPECIES

The Spanish or Iberian lynx once lived throughout Spain but now only a few hundred remain, mainly living in the Coto Doñana marshland reserve in southern Spain. This beautiful lynx has been reduced to near extinction by roads and agriculture destroying its natural habitat. It is now the world's most threatened cat species. Rare species like this can be protected by the preservation of their habitat, reducing any trade in their fur or other body parts, and captive breeding programmes.

GLOSSARY

Aestivation A summer hibernation, carried out in a cool place to escape high temperatures or drought.

Echolocation A way of locating objects by sending out sound waves and listening to the echo that comes back.

Ecosystem A community of living and non-living things which depend on each other for mutual survival.

Epiphyte A plant that grows on another plant for support, and lives off the nutrients from the air and rain.

Estuaries Places where freshwater rivers and streams flow into the ocean, mixing with the seawater.

Hydroelectric power Using the power of water flowing downwards to turn turbines and create electricity.

Invertebrate An animal that does not have a backbone, such as an ant.

Migration The movement of animals from one habitat to another according to the seasons.

Photosynthesis The process used by green plants to make food from light energy, carbon dioxide and water

Pollination The process where pollen is carried to a flower's reproductive organs (usually by insects) allowing the flower to produce seeds.

ACKNOWLEDGEMENTS

We would like to thank: Helen Wire and Elizabeth Wiggans for their assistance. Artwork by Peter Bull Art Studio.

Copyright © 2009 *ticktock* Entertainment Ltd

First published in Great Britain by *ticktock* Media Ltd, The Old Sawmill, 103 Goods Station Road, Tunbridge Wells, Kent TN1 2DP, Great Britain

All rights reserved. No part of this publication may be reproduced, stored in a retrieval system, or transmitted in any form or by any means electronic, mechanical, photocopying, recording or otherwise, without prior written permission of the copyright owner.

A CIP catalogue record for this book is available from the British Library.

ISBN 978 1 84898 002 0 (paperback)

ISBN 978 1 84898 049 5 (hardback)

Picture research by Image Select. Printed in China.

Picture Credits: t=top, b=bottom, c=centre, l=left, r=right, OFC=outside front cover, OBC=outside back cover, IFC=inside front cover

Oxford Scientific Films; 2ct, 2/3c, 3br, 3tr, 4tl, 4bl, 4/5t, 5cb, 6tl, 7br, 7c, 7cr, 8ct, 8/9c, 9t, 10bl, 10ct, 11cl, 12br, 13c, 16bl, 16/17t, 16/17b, 17cr, 17br, 18bl, 18tl, 19br, 19tr, 20/21b, 20/21b, 21cb, 22tl, 22c, 23b, 23tl, 23tr, 24cl, 24/25 (main pic), 25tr, 26/27b & OBCbl, 28ct, 30b, 30l, 30/31cb. Planet Earth Pictures; 24tl. Science Photo Library; 9b. Silvestris Fotoservice/FLPA; OFC. Still Pictures; 6/7t, 8l, 12/13t. Tony Stone; 12l, 28/29, 31br, IFC & 20tl, 2l, 3cr, 5cr, 10/11c, 12l, 13tr, 13br, 14bl, 14tl, 14c, 14/15c, 15br, 15r, 18/19, 18/19cb, 21c, 22bl, 24/25t, 26l, 27tr, 27c, 28bl, 28/29b, 28/29t, 30/31t & OBCbr, 31cr, 31b.

Every effort has been made to trace the copyright holders and we apologise in advance for any unintentional omissions. We would be pleased to insert the appropriate acknowledgement in any subsequent edition of this publication.